Time to Eat

MW00341334

Follow each path with a crayon.

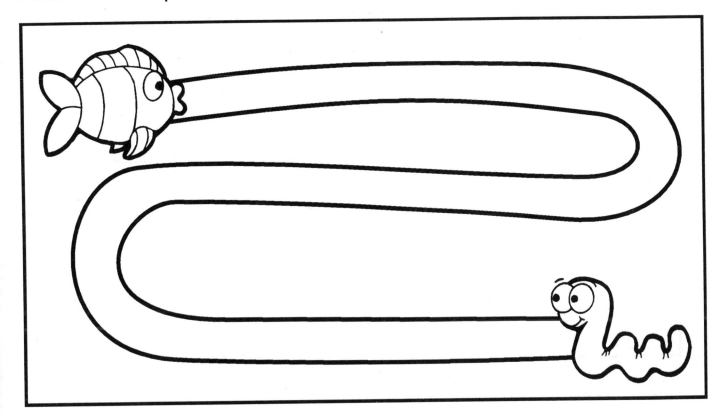

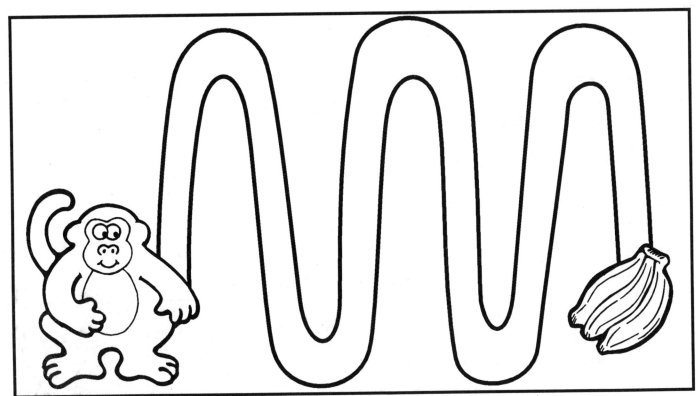

1

FS-32065 Beginning Modern Manuscript Handwriting

Going Home

Follow each path with a crayon.

2

FS-32065 Beginning Modern Manuscript Handwriting

Matching Shapes

Trace the lines from left to right.

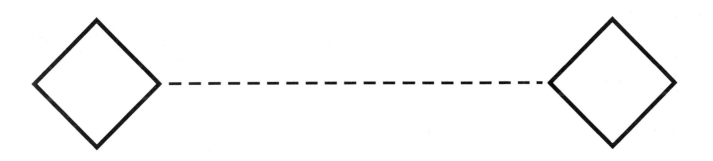

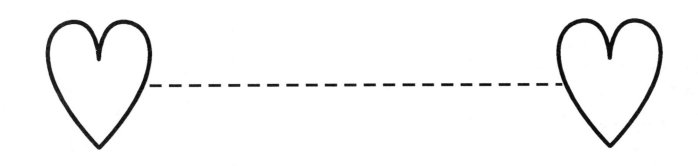

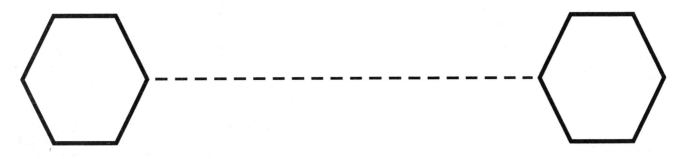

Playing Sports

Trace the lines from left to right.

4

On the Go

Trace the lines from left to right.

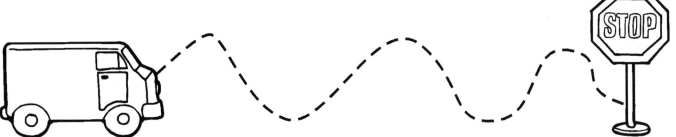

5

FS-32065 Beginning Modern Manuscript Handwriting

Find the Rhyme

Trace the lines from left to right.

Moving Along

Trace each line carefully. Do not lift your pencil until you get to the stop sign.

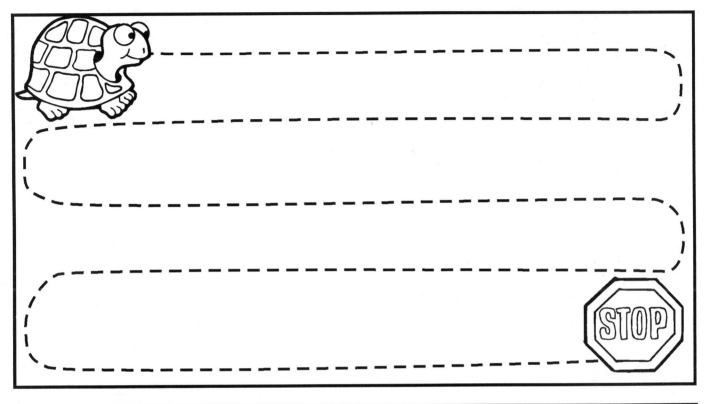

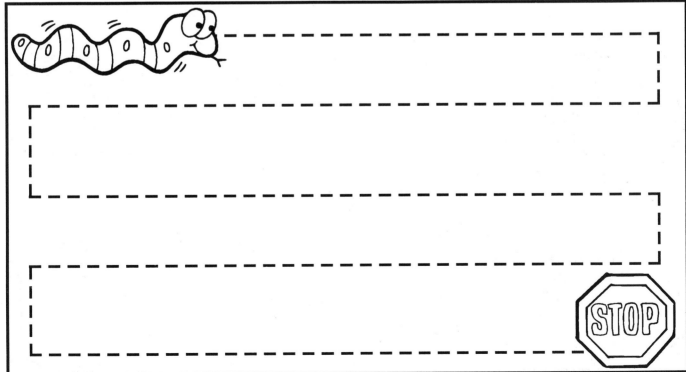

Flying South

Trace the lines from top to bottom.

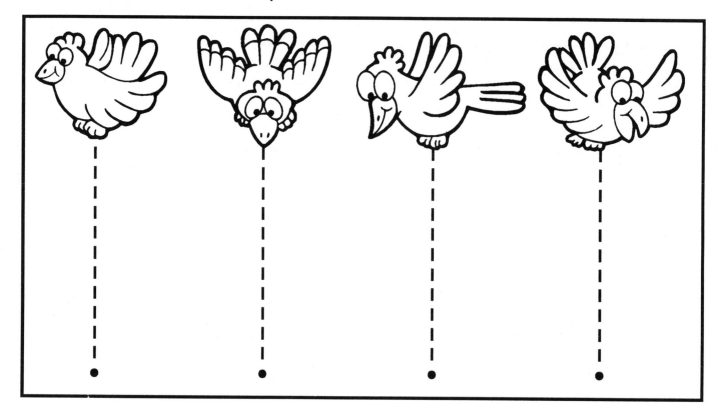

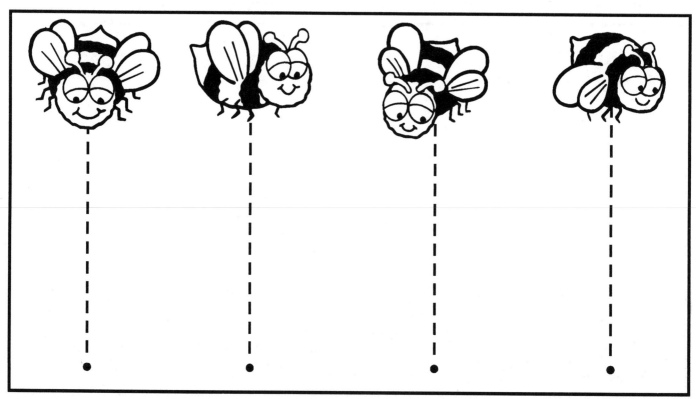

More Than One

Trace the lines from top to bottom.

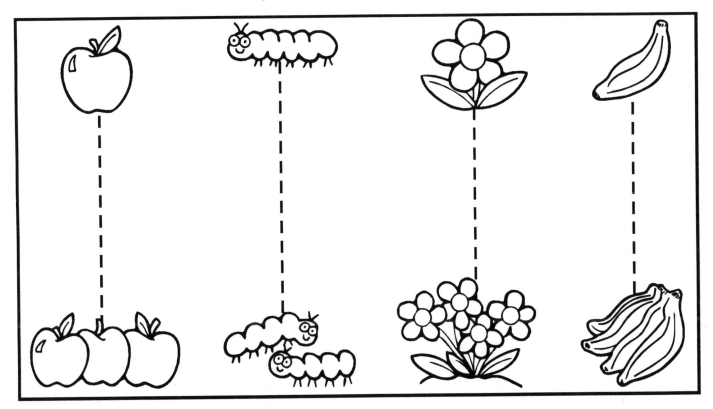

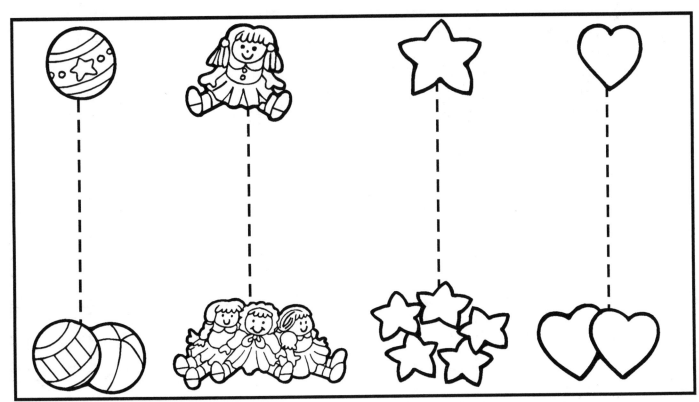

Follow the Path

Trace each line carefully. Do not lift your pencil until you get to the stop sign.

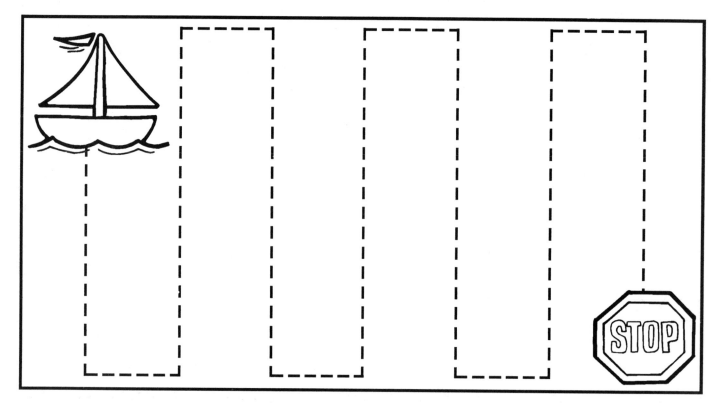

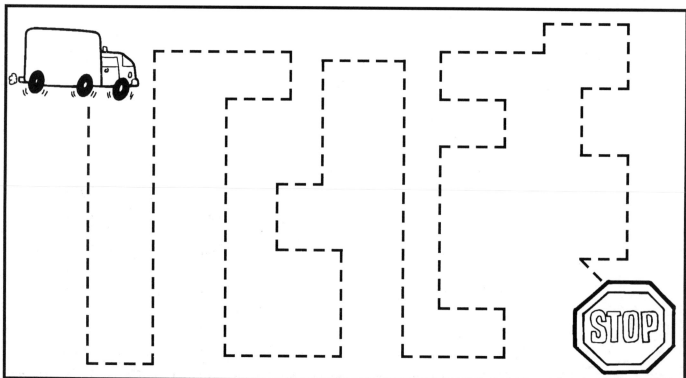

Circles

Trace the circles. Color the pictures.

Squares

Trace the squares. Color the pictures.

Triangles

Trace the triangles. Color the pictures.

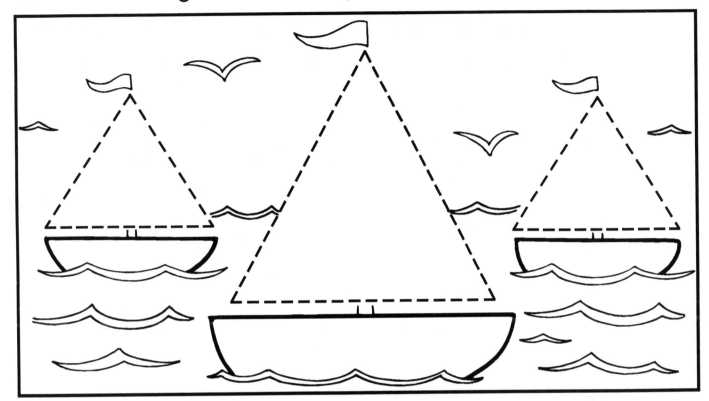

     FS-32065 Beginning Modern Manuscript Handwriting

Drawing Shapes

Trace the shapes. Draw each shape three times.

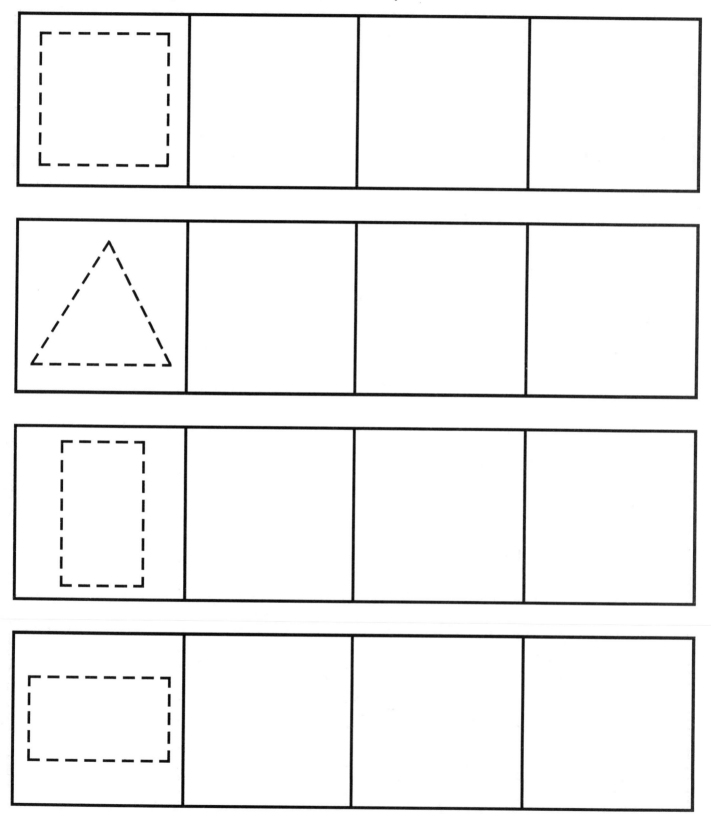

FS-32065 Beginning Modern Manuscript Handwriting

More Shapes

Trace the shapes. Draw each shape three times.

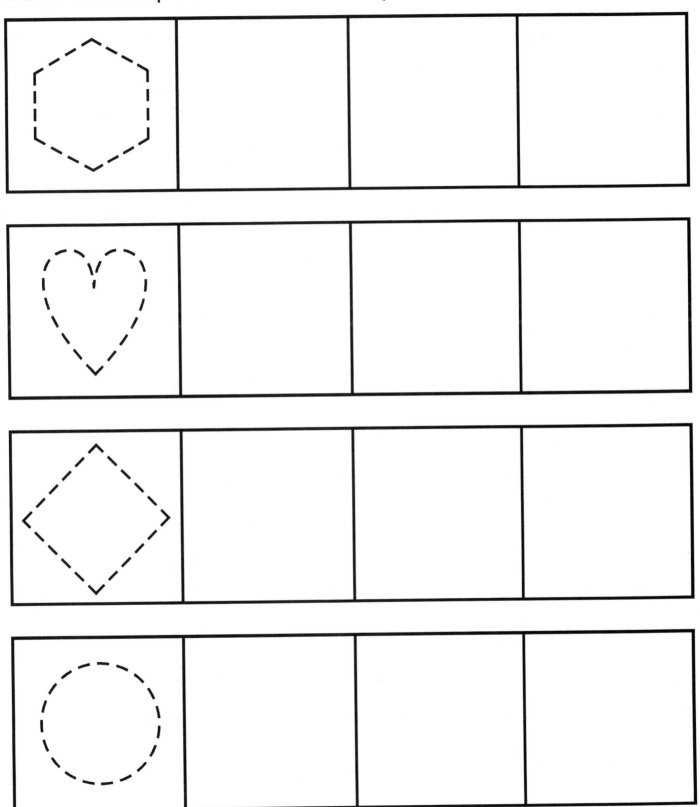

Connect the Dots

Copy the patterns shown.

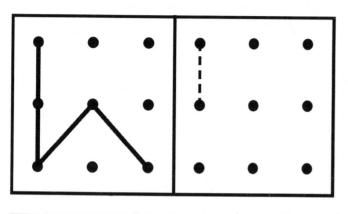

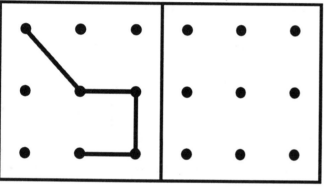

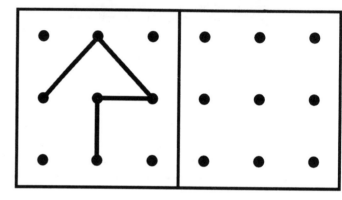

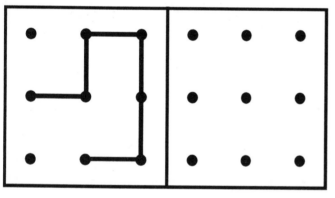

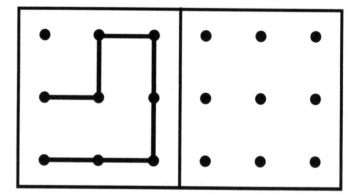

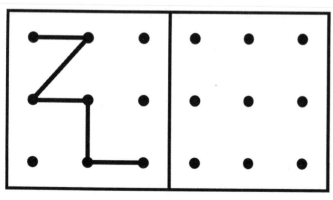

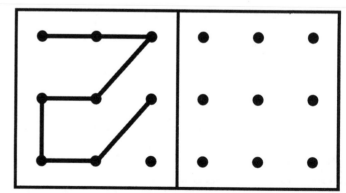

Find a Match

In each box, draw lines to match the pictures.

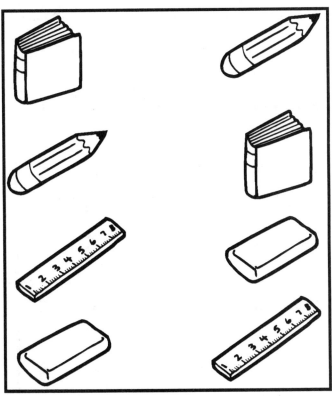

FS-32065 Beginning Modern Manuscript Handwriting

Tracing Aa and Bb

Tracing Cc and Dd

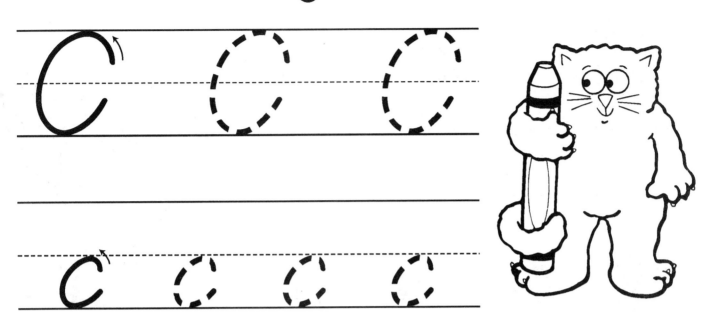

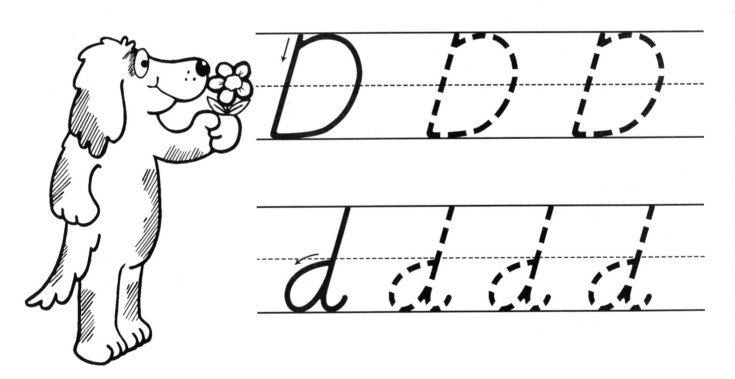

Tracing Ee and Ff

Tracing Gg and Hh

FS-32065 Beginning Modern Manuscript Handwriting

Tracing Ii and Jj

Tracing Kk and Ll

Name_____

Tracing Mm and Nn

Tracing Oo and Pp

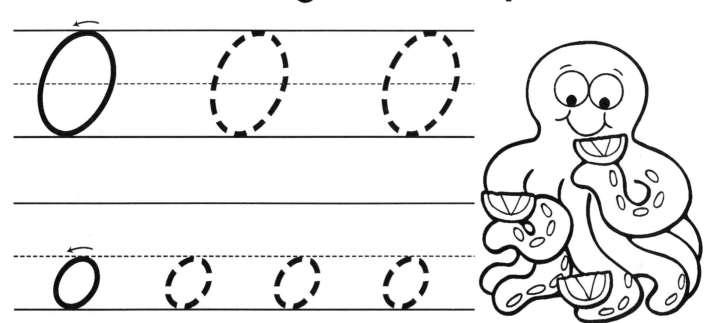

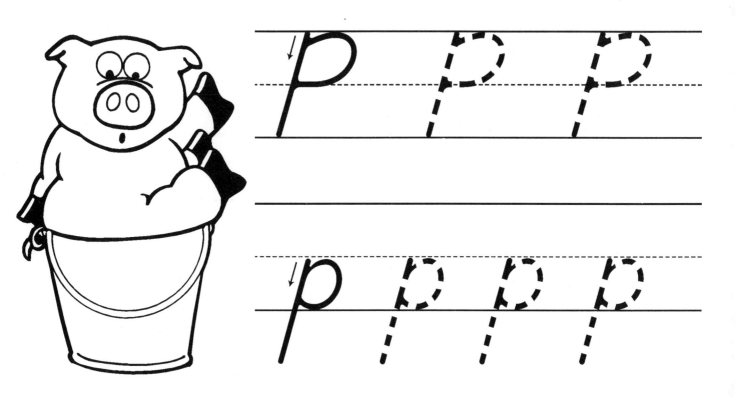

Tracing Qq and Rr

Q   Q   Q   Q

q   q   q   q

R   R   R   R

r   r   r   r

Tracing Ss and Tt

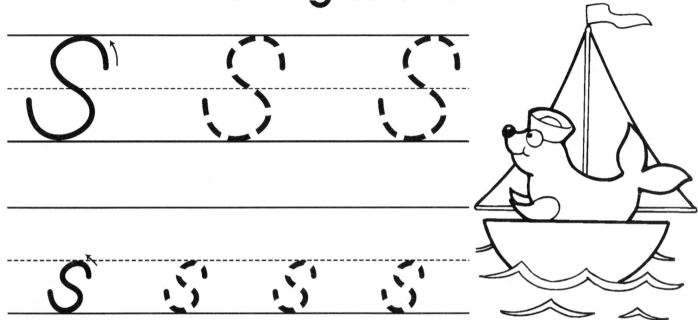

Tracing Uu and Vv

Tracing Ww and Xx

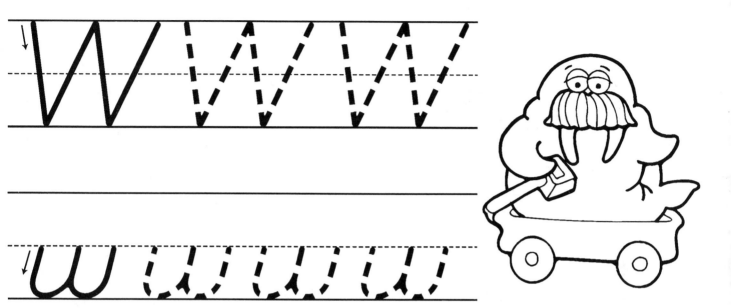

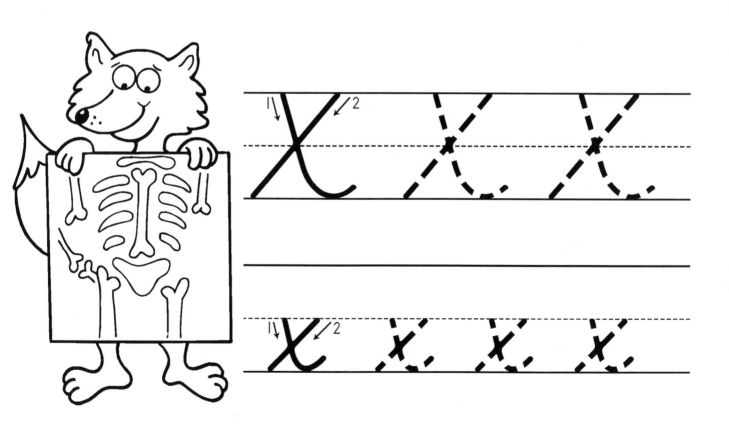

Tracing Yy and Zz

FS-32065 Beginning Modern Manuscript Handwriting

Tracing A to Z

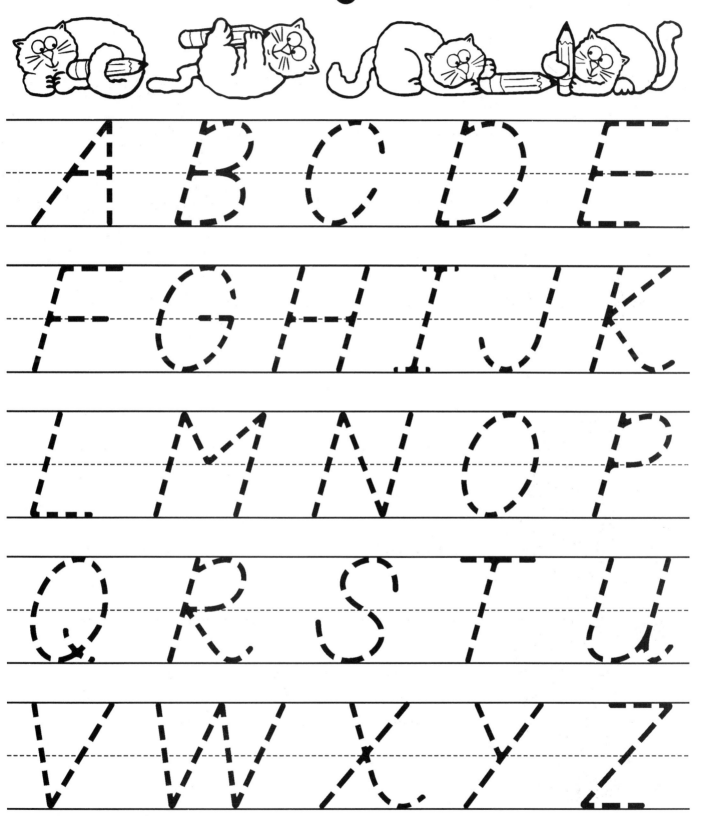

Tracing a to z

a b c d e f g

h i j k l m

n o p q r s t

u v w x y z

Aa

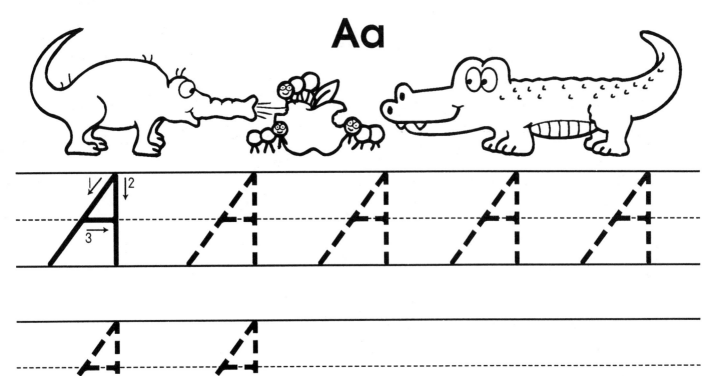

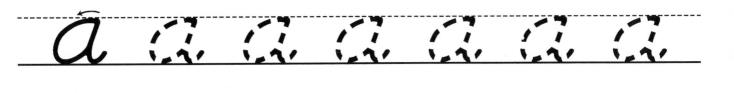

 FS-32065 Beginning Modern Manuscript Handwriting

Bb

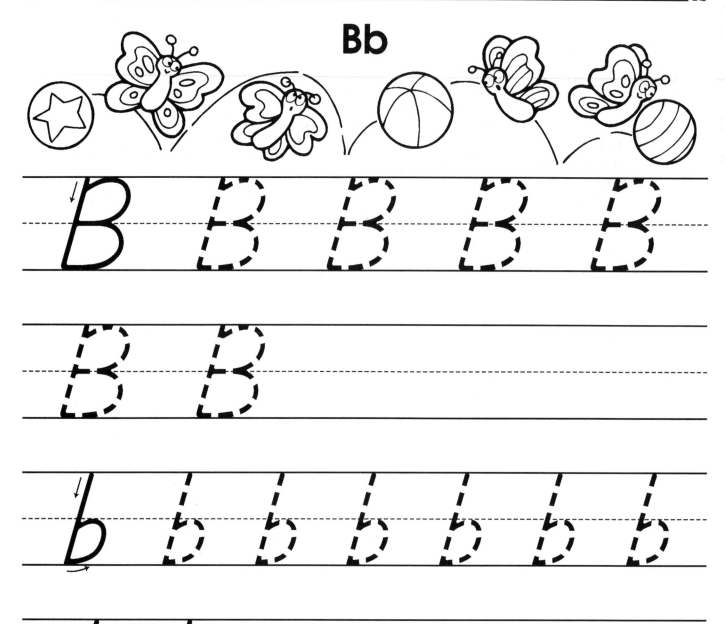

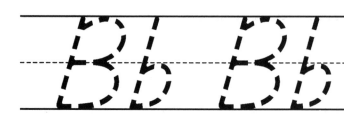

     FS-32065 Beginning Modern Manuscript Handwriting

Cc

C C C C C

C C

C C C C C C C

c c

c c

Dd

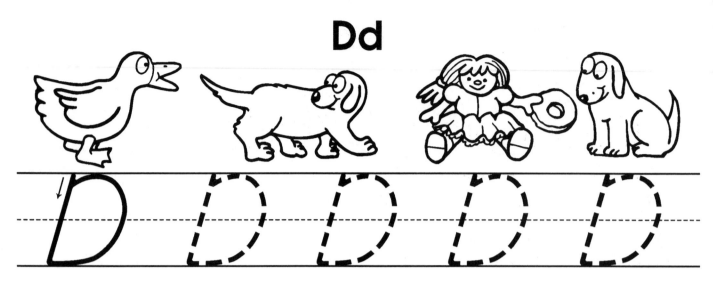

D D D D D

D D

d d d d d d d

d d

Da Da

Ee

E E E E E

E E

e e e e e e e

e e

Ee Ee

Ff

FS-32065 Beginning Modern Manuscript Handwriting

Gg

G G G G G

G G

g g g g g g g

g g

g g g g

Hh

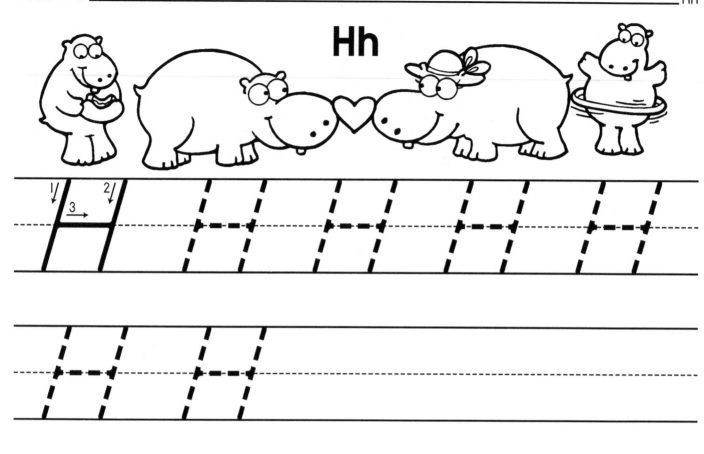

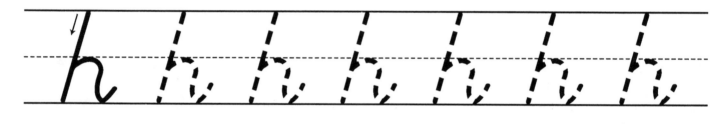

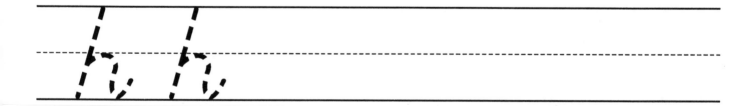

40

FS-32065 Beginning Modern Manuscript Handwriting

I

i

FS-32065 Beginning Modern Manuscript Handwriting

Jj

J

j

FS-32065 Beginning Modern Manuscript Handwriting

Kk

 FS-32065 Beginning Modern Manuscript Handwriting

Name _____

Ll

FS-32065 Beginning Modern Manuscript Handwriting

Mm

M M M M M M M

M M M

m m m m m m m m

m m

Mm Mm

Nn

N N N N N

N N

n n n n n n n

n n

N N

46

Oo

O O O O O

O O

O o o o o o o

o o

O o O o

Pp

P P P P P P

P P

p p p p p p

p p

P p

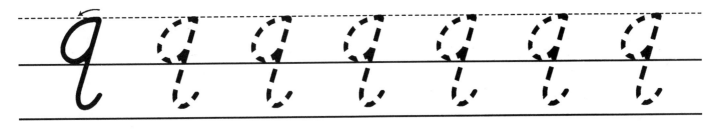

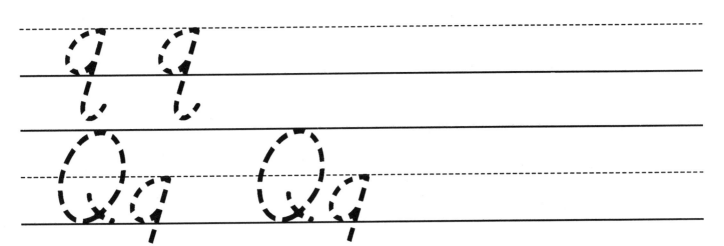

FS-32065 Beginning Modern Manuscript Handwriting

Rr

R R R R R

R R

r r r r r

r r

R R R

Ss

Name _____ Tt

Tt

Uu

U U U U U

U U

U u u u u u u

u u

Uu Uu

Vv

54

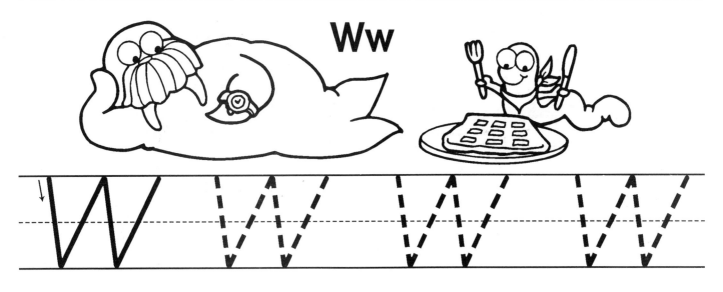

Ww

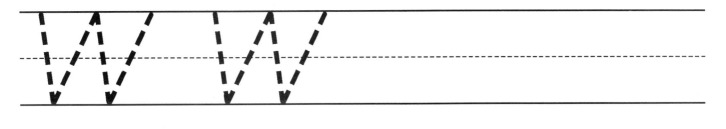

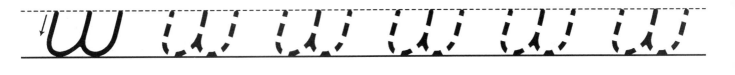

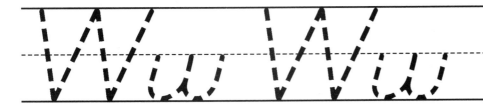

Xx

FS-32065 Beginning Modern Manuscript Handwriting

Yy

Y Y Y Y Y

Y Y

y y y y y y y

Zz

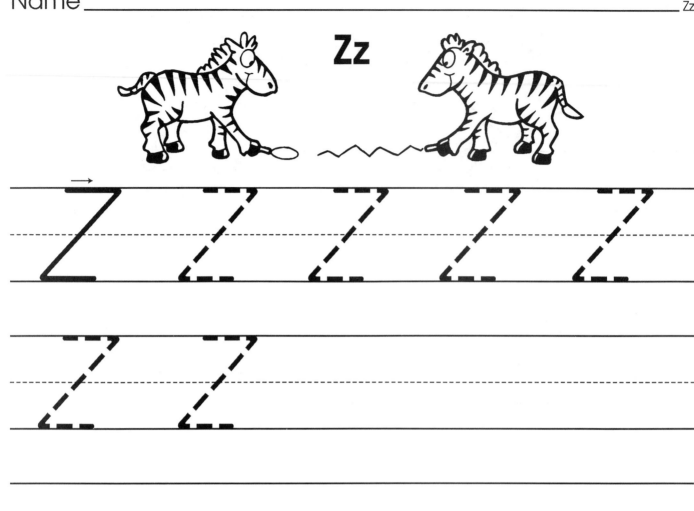

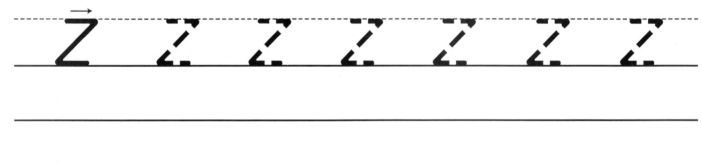

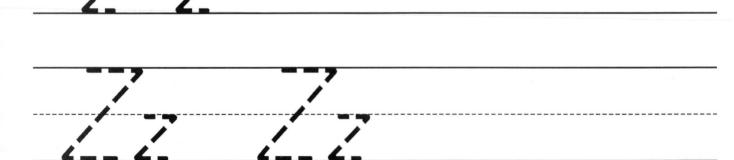

Name

Let's Count

FS-32065 Beginning Modern Manuscript Handwriting

Name_____

More Counting

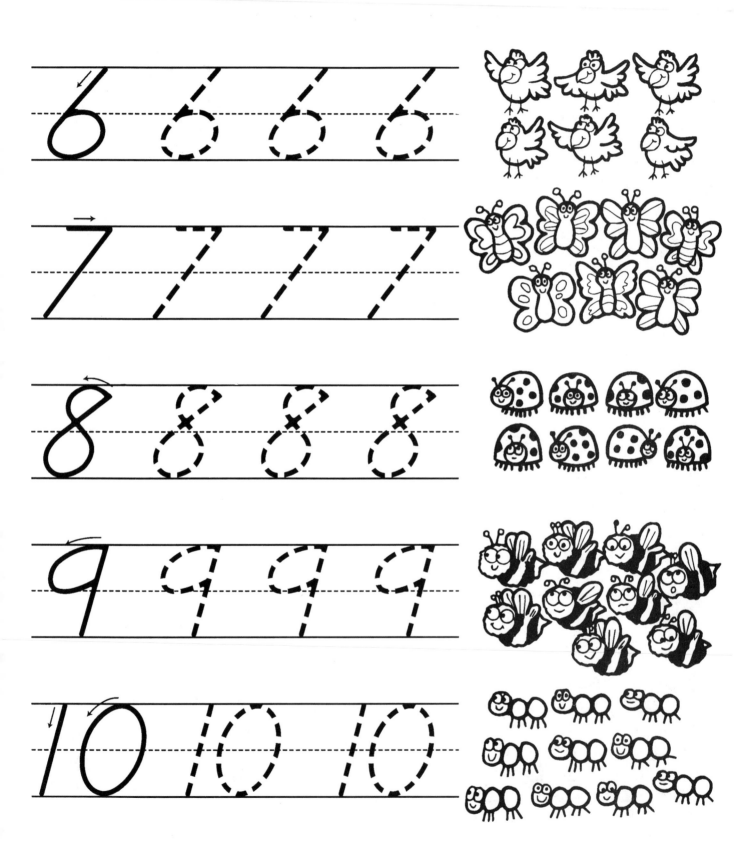

Busy Butterflies

Trace the letters. Match the capital letters to the lowercase letters.

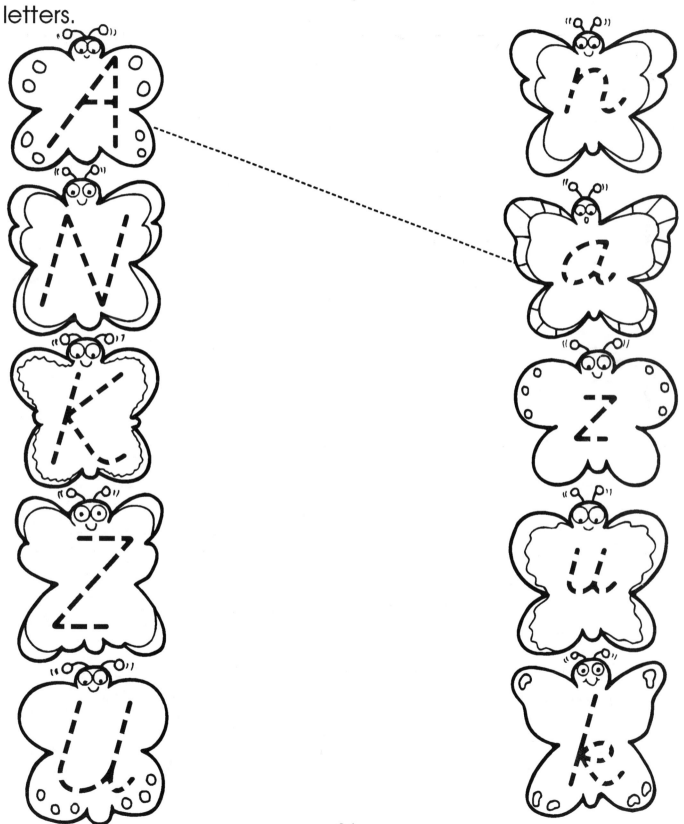

Friendly Fish

Trace the letters. Match the capital letters to the lowercase letters.

Hats for You

Write the matching lowercase letters.

A a

H

N

X

B

K

G

C

Wiggly Worms

Write the matching capital letters.

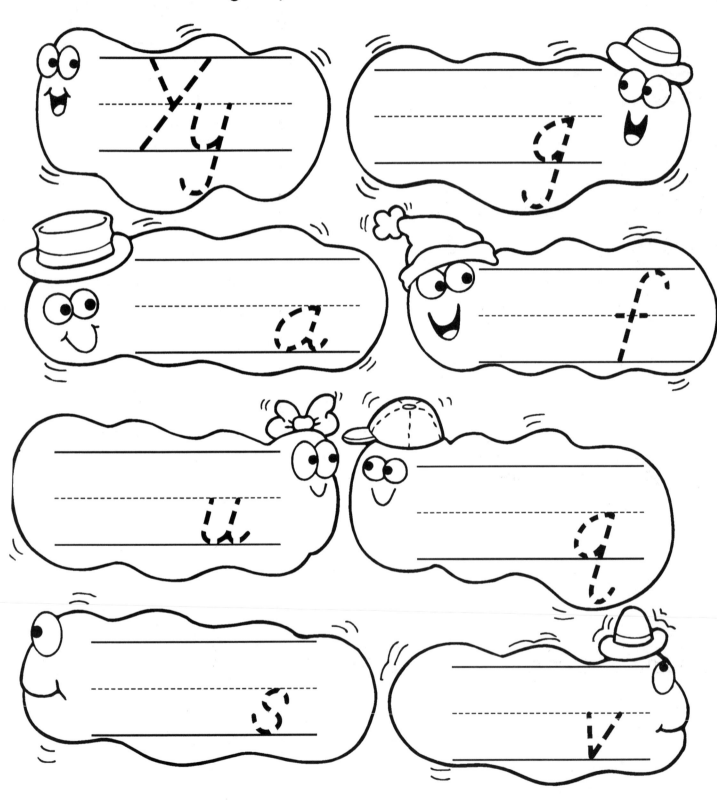

FS-32065 Beginning Modern Manuscript Handwriting

Aa

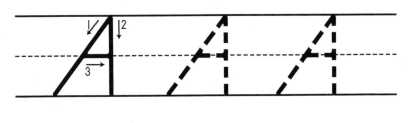

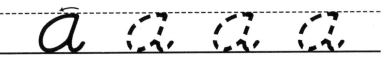

Anna

Alex

ant

apple

65

Bb

B B B

b b b b

Billy

Brenda

bear

boot

Cc

C c c

c c c c

Carrie

Chris

camel

cake

FS-32065 Beginning Modern Manuscript Handwriting

Dd

D D D D

d d d d

David

Dana

door

dinosaur

Ee

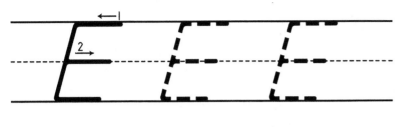

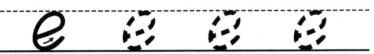

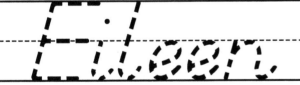

Eileen.

egg

eagle

Ff

F F F F

f f f f

Fran

Fred

frog

flower

Gg

G G G

g g g g

Gina

Greg

gorilla

grape

71

FS-32065 Beginning Modern Manuscript Handwriting

Hh

H H H H H

h h h h

Hayley

Hank

hat

hen

Ii

I I I I

i i i i

Isaac

Irene

iron

iguana

Jj

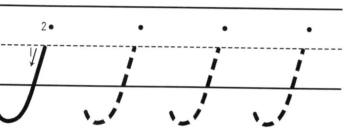

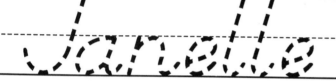

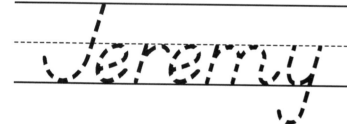

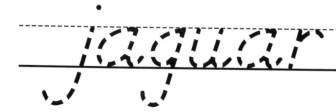

Janelle

Jeremy

jet

jaguar

FS-32065 Beginning Modern Manuscript Handwriting

Kk

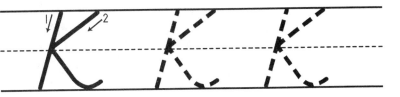

FS-32065 Beginning Modern Manuscript Handwriting

LI

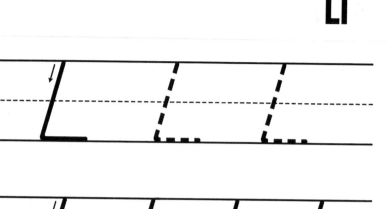

Leo

Lydia

lion

letter

Mm

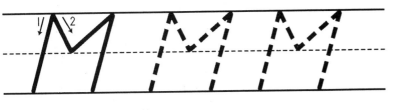

Marco

Mimi

monkey

map

Nn

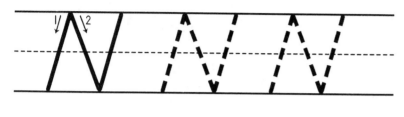

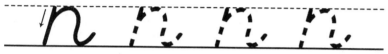

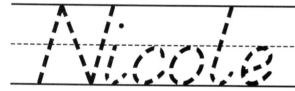

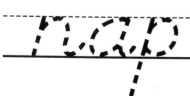

78

FS-32065 Beginning Modern Manuscript Handwriting

Oo

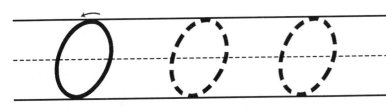

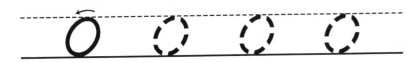

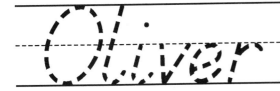

Olga

Oliver

orange

owl

Pp

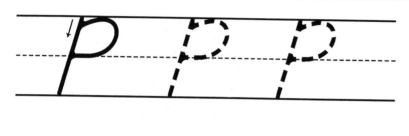

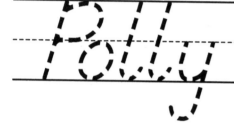

Polly

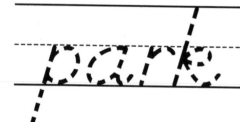

Pedro

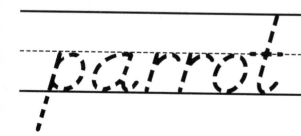

park

parrot

FS-32065 Beginning Modern Manuscript Handwriting

Qq

Q Q Q

q q q q

Quincy

Quiana

quail

quilt

Rr

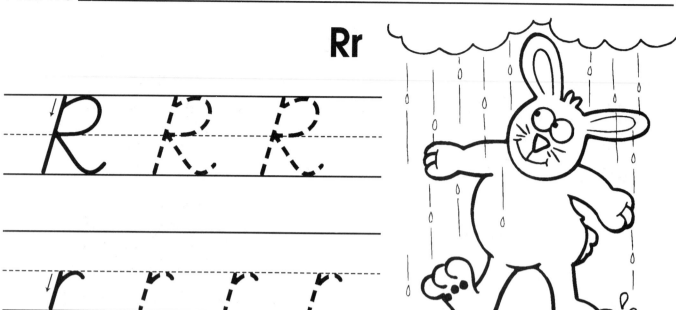

R R R R

r r r r

Rosa

Robert

rain

rabbit

Name_____

Ss

S S S

s s s s

Sergio

Sara

star

snake

FS-32065 Beginning Modern Manuscript Handwriting

Tt

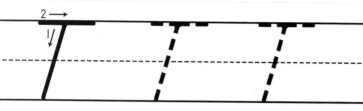

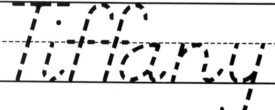

Tony

Tiffany

tent

tiger

Uu

U U U

u u u u

Ursula

Ulysses

under

unicorn

    FS-32065 Beginning Modern Manuscript Handwriting

Vv

Vera

Victor

vulture

vest

86

Ww

Ww Www

w w w w w

Wayne

Wendy

walrus

watch

FS-32065 Beginning Modern Manuscript Handwriting

Xx

X x x x

x x x x

Xavier

Xena

x-ray

xylophone

Yy

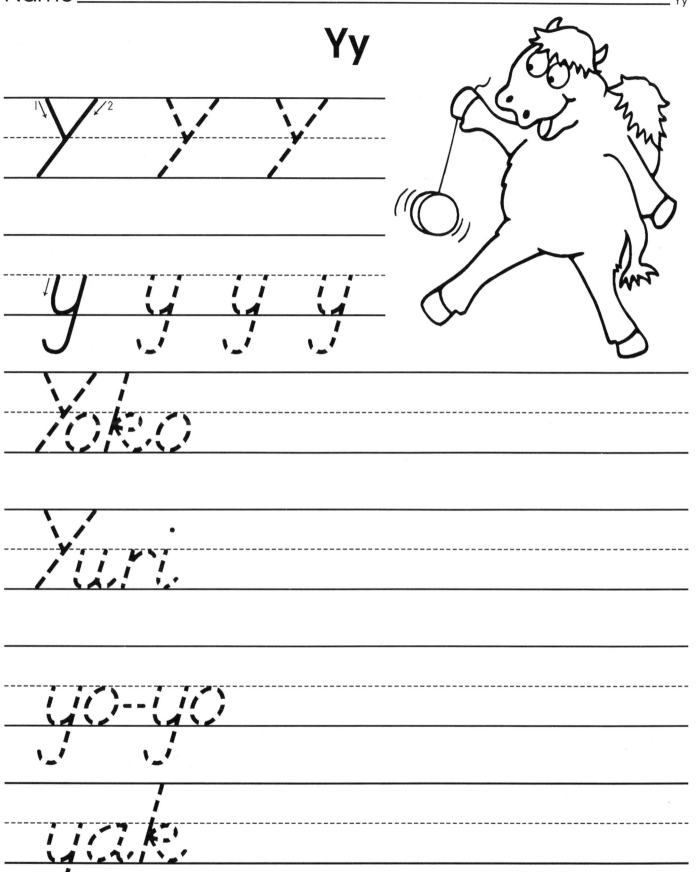

Y Y Y Y

y y y y

Yoko

Yuri

yo-yo

yak

89

Zz

Z Z Z Z

z z z z z

Zoe

Zane

zipper

zebra

What's Missing?

Write the capital letters in order.

A ___ ___ D ___

___ G ___ I J

K ___ M ___ ___

___ O ___ ___ T

U ___ W ___ ___

___ Y ___

Writing a to z

Write the lowercase letters in order.

  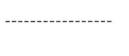 

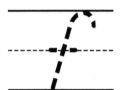 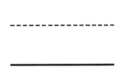 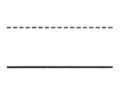 

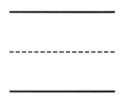  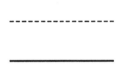 

  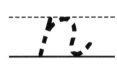 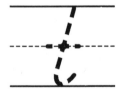

 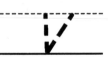 

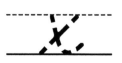 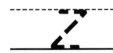 

92

Name_____

Numbers 0–5

0

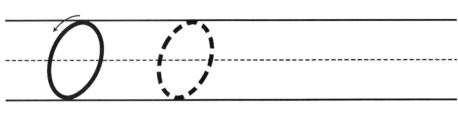

1

2

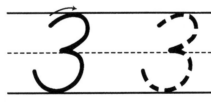

3

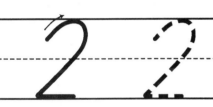

4

5

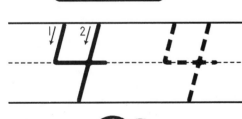

93

Name_____

Numbers 6–10

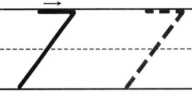

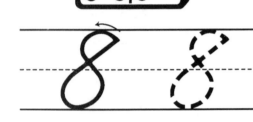

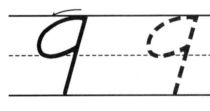

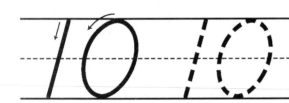

Write your phone number below.

_____

FS-32065 Beginning Modern Manuscript Handwriting

Number Words

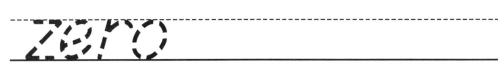

zero

one

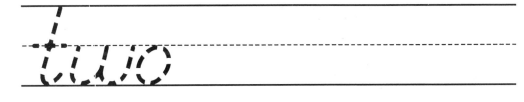

two

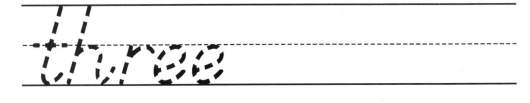

three

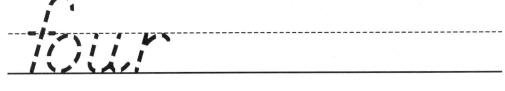

four

five

FS-32065 Beginning Modern Manuscript Handwriting

More Number Words

six

seven

eight

nine

ten

FS-32065 Beginning Modern Manuscript Handwriting

Aa

A a

Aaron

apples

Aaron ate apples.

Bb

My Best

Bb

bees

buzz

Busy bees buzz.

Cc

Cc

cats

cakes

Cats cut cakes.

Dd

D d

My Best

ducks

dive

Ducks dive deep.

Name_____

Ee

My Best

Ee

Erin

eggs

Erin eats eggs.

FS-32065 Beginning Modern Manuscript Handwriting

Ff

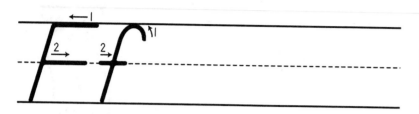

foxes

fish

Five foxes fish.

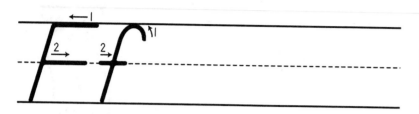

Gg

My Best

Gg

goats

golfing

Goats go golfing.

© Frank Schaffer Publications, Inc.   FS-32065 Beginning Modern Manuscript Handwriting

Hh

My Best

Hh

hens

hats

Hens have hats.

FS-32065 Beginning Modern Manuscript Handwriting

Ii

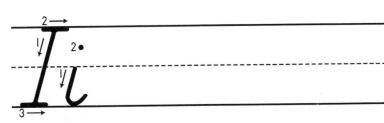

My Best

Ivan

Italy

Is Ivan in Italy?

Jj

My Best

Jj

Jim

juggles

Jim juggles jars.

Kk

K k

Katie

kick

Kangaroos kick.

Ll

My Best

Ll

Lindsay

laughs

Lindsay laughs.

Mm

My Best

M m

Meg

mud

Meg mixes mud.

Nn

My Best

Nn

Natalie

nibbles

Natalie nibbles.

Oo

My Best

Oo

Otto

oboes

Otto owns oboes.

FS-32065 Beginning Modern Manuscript Handwriting

Pp

Pp

Paul

poppies

Paul picks poppies.

FS-32065 Beginning Modern Manuscript Handwriting

Name _____

Qq

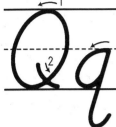

Q q

queens

quilt

Queens quilt.

FS-32065 Beginning Modern Manuscript Handwriting

Rr

My Best

Rr

rats

races

Rats run races.

Ss

My Best

Ss

Sue

soup

Sue sips soup.

Tt

My Best

Tt

turtles

tiptoe

Turtles tiptoe.

116

Uu

My Best

Uu

umpires

unite

Umpires unite.

Vv

My Best

V v

Violet

Vern

Violet visits Vern.

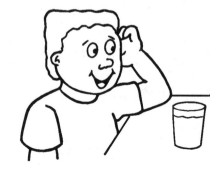

FS-32065 Beginning Modern Manuscript Handwriting

Ww

My Best

Ww

Wanda

worries

Wanda worries.

Xx

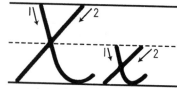

My Best

Xavier

x-rays

Xavier x-rays x's.

120

FS-32065 Beginning Modern Manuscript Handwriting

Yy

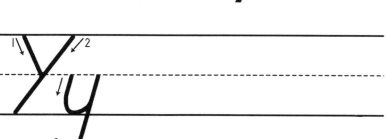

Y y

Yvette

yawns

Yvette yawns.

Zz

My Best

Z z

Zach

zippers

Zach zips zippers.

Days of the Week

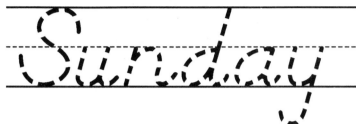

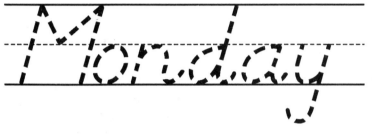

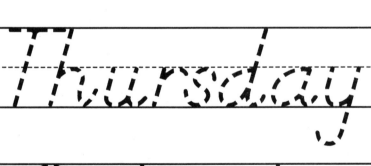

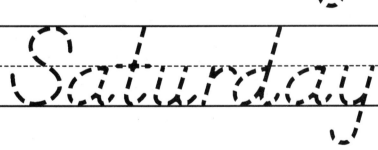

Today is
_____

_____

Months of the Year

January

February

March

April

May

June

Months of the Year

July

August

September

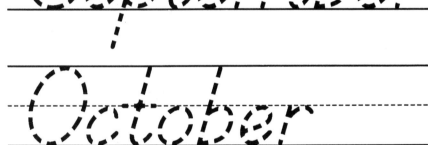

October

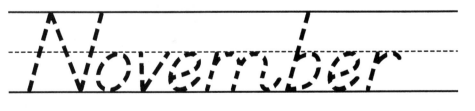

November

December

FS-32065 Beginning Modern Manuscript Handwriting

Name_____

Colors

 *red*

 *blue*

 *green*

 *purple*

 *yellow*

 *orange*

 *black*

What's My Name?

Write your first and last names in your very best handwriting.

Draw a picture of you practicing your handwriting.

All the Letters

Copy this sentence neatly. It contains
every letter of the alphabet.

The quick

brown fox jumps

over the lazy dog.